Girl,

Go For It

The Single Black Woman's Blueprint to Living
Life Fearlessly

Shannon Wilkerson

Dedication

To my mother, aunties, sisters, cousins, and sister friends, we have been through some things and still walked away with our superpowers intact.

We always win!

To my daughters, you are a constant reminder that God honors His promises.

Table of Contents

Fearless; without fear, bold, brave, and intrepid.

Introduction

I remember being unhappy with where my life was going, and coming to the realization that I was the only one who could change it. Things weren't terrible. I had a degree, a successful career in education, a training and consulting business on the side, a few dollars in the bank etc. My situation was good. I just absolutely knew that I was not where God had called me to be. If you have ever been in that place, you know that it comes with a feeling of empty space on the inside. You may not even know where the feeling is coming from. You just know that something isn't right. I knew that there was more! Why was I not experiencing more?

I took a deep dive into my own thoughts and patterns and realized that I wasn't experiencing more because I wasn't doing what was necessary to get it. I wasn't boldly stepping out on faith like I should have been or seeking advancement opportunities. I was comfortable. I got in my comfort zone and reclined my seat. That's where I was. I had to get myself out of what was familiar and start living like God had a plan for me, because He did. Where should I begin, though? What were my next steps? What should I do with this plan that God had for me?

God creates the plan, but we must work at it to walk in it. Some of us just sit with it, pondering what to do year after year. Even then, it does not go to waste. It just doesn't produce for us. If you don't work the plan, someone else will because there is still a need for that gift in the earth. God is still going to see the fruit of it, by way of you or someone else. Let's get to a place where it is through us. Stop missing out on the big things that God is doing sis! Take your rightful place! Get in position!

Single, black woman, you can do all that God has planned for you and be all that He has called you to be, and guess what, you don't need a spouse to help you do it! All you need is fearlessness, faith, and a plan! This is not a man bashing book. I do desire marriage with a fine black man with chocolate skin and pretty white teeth. I just wasn't willing to sit around waiting for him to save me or to help me to fulfil what God planned for me. Now, when I do get married, I will be marrying as a whole person who has achieved some of my life goals, while learning some life lessons in the journey. This will benefit, not just me, but my future husband also.

I encourage you to absorb what is within these pages. After all, I wrote this book for you, girl! I'm sure that you will be able to relate to parts of my journey. The other parts, you can share with a friend. She needs it too!

I hope that reading my story mixed with some sisterly advice will make you feel less alone and more capable. Designing your life is up to you. Dealing with the fear that holds you back is up to you. You have to decide how you want to live from this day forward. Whatever your decisions include, know that God is with you all the way. So, there's nothing left to do but go for it!

Chapter One

Creating the Narrative

The way that we choose to do life, establishes how others view our lives. We know to not get caught up in opinions, critics, and how others see us. However, there are times when that does matter. For example, I care about how my daughters view me. It is important to me that they see me as a successful woman. That's the only way they'll be able to see themselves that way in the earliest stages of their lives. I care about how other young black girls see me. I have lived enough life and had enough experiences to know that for some of them, seeing me successful may be the only positive example of a black woman that they see up close and personal. Seeing people on tv doesn't count.

Success and how we define it, is different for everyone, but there are some things that are pretty standard. Those things include being able to do what you love, being happy and at peace with yourself, and making a positive impact on others. We need to show young black girls what that can look like. We also need to teach them that they can decide what success means to them. We need to create our own narrative and teach them to do the same, especially if they are our own children. We should be passing on more than debt. For those of us who have the necessary financial things in order, you need to pass on more than money. It's not enough. Our children need to know how to live a satisfying existence. Otherwise, all the money in the world doesn't do much for them.

When we don't take a leadership role in creating our own narrative, we allow someone else to do so. People will be quick to paint an inaccurate picture of you, what you're like, and what you can be, do and have. In fact, they will jump at the chance to write your story. We need to get ahead of that and paint our own picture. How do you do that? Seek God on His plans for your life and ask Him how to map it out. He will show you! The question is, can you follow instructions? That is key. Many people go to God in prayer. Not all listen and obey.

When I started to strategize my next moves that would help me to align with His plan, I didn't fully know the plan. I just knew that I was safest within that plan and that it would require faith over fear. I would have never guessed that I would have ended up where I am now. I'll get more into that as I continue on. For now, I just want to stress that we must be open to new experiences, even those that are uncomfortable, unfamiliar, and cause us to stretch a bit. You may find yourself on one step and not know what is ahead. Just trust that it will be revealed and keep going.

When you look over your life, can you identify times when you allowed someone else's idea of you to shape your actions? Did someone have expectations of you that caused you to go in one direction when you should have gone the other way? Have you held back utilizing your gifts because you were afraid of how you would be received? It's not just you. If it were just you, I wouldn't be writing a whole book about it. These are normal occurrences. Let's normalize doing it anyway, doing it scared, and going where we know we should be. Turn off the noise, that is other people and get your focus back.

Your story matters. It matters so much that somebody needs it to live a better life themselves. Sometimes people need permission to make strides. They feel like if they do well, other people will be jealous, judge them, use them, take from them, or even try to sabotage them. The sad part is that all of that is true. People will do those things, but they ultimately can't hurt you and even those situations will help you to grow and develop. What they meant to use to harm you, will be turned around to work in your favor. No, it won't feel good in the moment. There are real feelings that surface when people hurt us. We just have to dust ourselves off and keep our eyes on the end result.

There will always be efforts made to silence you so that old false narratives can be put out there. It may make you feel like you must work twice as hard to squash those narratives and to recreate one that will put you in a better light. You don't. Their story about you is their business and their problem. Your only focus should be being the best you. Don't stress about what other people are doing, The truth will always shine through. This is something that I am teaching my daughters. Of course, at their young ages, they struggle with it, but the seed has been planted. So, as they grow and encounter these scenarios, they will know how to handle themselves.

What I want most for my girls, and every little brown girl, is to be confident enough to live in their truth and by their own standard. They need not live how someone else dictates or based on the box that someone wants to put them in. I want them to be courageous enough to write their own story and tell it boldly! They have gifts on the inside of them. To cultivate those gifts and bring them forward, they must have examples of women who are doing just that. It's important that those women are us. We look like them. We represent them. We are them!

Has anyone ever told you that you wouldn't amount to anything? I hear that, and even worse so often from young black girls. Fortunately, I didn't have to live that. I didn't have parents who talked down to me or allowed other people to do so. I was encouraged and uplifted at home. My mom wasn't cursing me out. She wasn't on drugs, an alcoholic or anything even close. If your upbringing was very different from mine, its ok. You can do this too! You can recreate your own story and be something totally different from your mother. You don't have to hold onto what she did, who she was or who she may still be. That's her business. At this point, it has nothing to do with you.

Maybe you are one of the parents who were raised that way and in turn, began addressing your children that way. Know that you are creating a negative storyline for them. However, it is never too late to change that. At any time, you can apologize to those children for how you have added to their story and start adding in new and better ways. It doesn't have to be that you were terrible. Maybe you just fuss too much. I was guilty of that until I realized how it affected my children.

One day I was just looking at my daughters and how innocent they were, and how much they relied on me for love, comfort, and safety. It's obviously important to teach and create discipline. However, gentle parenting does work, for the most part. It may not always work perfectly and may not be the easiest route, but I can tell you that it's much more effective than hitting children for everything that they do or worse. Older people will tell you that you talk to those kids too much, you need to spank them, they are getting over on you and running your house etc. Just keep in mind that the way that you raise your children will come back on you, not on those with opinions.

One thing I don't want is for my children to be afraid of me. People tell stories of how their parents used to handle them like it's a badge of honor. I hear it, like it's a horror story. I got spankings, but I don't recall ever really being afraid of my mother. I don't recall ever feeling like I couldn't go to her with an issue because I was going to get in trouble. Children don't have to be afraid of you to respect and honor you. I think that is where so many of us get this wrong. In the black community, we were taught that our kids should fear us. Thank God not all black parents bought into this.

My mother didn't play with us when it came to certain things, but she was still "mommy". I was always safe with her. I didn't want feelings of being unsafe to be a part of my children's narrative. I worked hard to establish trust with them. They know that I am always on their team and they should always tell me the truth so that we could work out the problem together. Then I fell into a habit of fussing and had to fix that with them. I couldn't say one thing and then let my actions say another. How could they trust that? It's so easy to confuse children when we operate in confusion. I didn't want that for them, and I know you don't want that for your children either.

My relationship with my girls has always been very positive. I believe I have successfully positioned myself to be their number one "go to" person for any and everything. I created that relationship by not dealing with them harshly when they make mistakes, showing them that I have their back, acting quickly when something in their environment is bothering them, showing and teaching love, etc. Even if you don't have children, you can be this person to someone. I believe in raising the next generation of brown girls (and boys) with an advantage in life. That does not only apply to my own children.

I know it can be a challenge to model for your children what was not modeled for you. Though that wasn't my experience, I get it. However, I do believe that you can break that generational curse and start a new thing with your babies, therefore changing the course of their lives. What you don't want is for your children to become adults who have feelings towards you that mimic those that you have for your mother if she wasn't the best. Don't be your children's bad memories. The outside world is difficult enough. It's your job to set a foundation that teaches them how to manage the stress of the world, not to be the stress of the world.

Committing To Yourself

Naturally, we want to do better for our children, right? What about doing better for you, though? We can't take ourselves out of the equation. Before those children came along, we mattered, and we still do! Parenting is a wonderful thing, and we should give it our best. We just have to know how to do that without

Don't be your children's bad memories!

giving it all of us. Somebody just fainted, I know! You can't believe I just said to not give your amazing children all of you!

Listen, I put my absolute best into raising my children daily. However, I save some for me too. That is super hard to do, especially as a single parent. You have to try, though, because if you don't, you're going to fail yourself and end up failing them anyway. You can find a way to still be you, while being their mother. It is one of the most important things you can do for them because you'll be happier. If you're happier, you'll be better at parenting.

What do you most enjoy about life, outside of the little people who live in your house? Why aren't you doing more of that? Do you even go outside? I'm not talking about going to work or taking them to gymnastics practice. I mean going out, taking yourself to dinner or even going on a date. You can still live! You can date and parent, just don't do them at the same time. It sounds funny, but hopefully, you know what I mean. You can't have any and everybody around your children. They must be protected both physically and emotionally. I will get into dating in a later chapter.

Maybe you don't have children yet, your children are adults, or you don't ever want children. You may have something else keeping you from committing to yourself. Have you given in to the lie that you can't do whatever it is that you want to do? Have you failed at it in the past? Is your confidence damaged? Whatever it is, you must identify it and then change it. One thing is certain. The only thing holding you back is you. That's what it all boils down to no matter the situation. Most excuses can be overcome. Most things, you can get up from. It's just a matter of wanting it more than you want to sit in your mess.

Many people will find that their issue is mindset. Because I know the importance of having the correct mindset, I am going to stay right there for a moment. First of all, you can have whatever you believe and say. Let's be clear about that! The Bible tells us this in Mark 11:23 and Pastor Cynthia Brazelton, wrote a whole book about it. I encourage you to read *"The Voice of Faith: Whosoever Can Have Whatsoever They Say!"* What are you saying? What are you speaking over your life? What are you believing about your life? It all matters and creates your circumstances. If you truly desire to create something else, say something else and believe it.

Your thinking is the key component to your believing, speaking, and doing. You will never do what you can't believe you can do, and you will never have what you don't believe you can have. What you will do, however, is watch other people have and do amazing things because they say it and believe it. We're going to get that together now, so that won't be your story. This is going to require that you first settle in your heart that God is for you and that He is more powerful than anything that stands in your way. If you know that much, how can you believe anything other than you can do all things? God is for you! Let that sink in and stand on it!

The only way to truly change the way that you think is to replace your thoughts with His. In other words, you must have the mind of Christ. Otherwise, that old way of thinking will creep right back in. It's still there under what you try to convince yourself in your own strength, without fully believing. Fixing this takes commitment because it involves doing the work. So, first decide that you are worth this work, and you are going to commit to doing it. Once you've established that, you're ready! Let's take on the world!

Sit down with pen and paper because we're about to get serious. Reflect on all the negative talk that goes on in your head. Write down those words. Then go back and replace those words with something positive. I learned this strategy as a teacher. We replaced negative talk for positive affirmations in working with parents and children to help them to establish a better mindset. You can put scripture here or even your own positive words. If you think, "I can't go back to school at my age because it will be too difficult" Replace that with "I will go back to school and be successful in obtaining a degree." This one is so real to me. I went back to school at forty something. So far, I'm maintaining a 4.00 with one year to completion.

Go down your whole list of negative thoughts and replace them all with thoughts that are going to cause you to take actions towards elevating. Get rid of all the thoughts that will cause you to think less of yourself. The work has begun! Now, you must remind yourself of these new thoughts whenever you think about that thing that you want to do and start taking the appropriate actions towards getting those things done. Stay prayed up too. Remember, we have an adversary, and his job is to kill, steal and destroy. Always be ready for combat!

Take a deep breath! That was probably emotional and hard to do, but you did it! You didn't do it because I said to do it. You did it because you are committed to yourself, your life, and your goals. You did it because you were determined to not let the fear of facing this list of negative thoughts hold you back from advancing to your next level. You did it because you realized the consequence of not doing it! I'm proud of you sis! It's important for me to say that because I know that some of you may not hear that from anyone else. Keep going anyway. Don't let a lack of support keep you from moving forward.

Committing to and working on being the best version of yourself can be uncomfortable at times. This is especially true if you've been trained to think that putting all this effort into yourself isn't necessary or that it won't make a difference. Other people tell us a bunch of lies. Negative experiences feed us a bunch of lies. We must rise above it. Though a negative experience is real and may even teach us something, we can learn the lesson and not stay in that moment. Don't get caught in the cycle of reliving a negative thing. Practice bouncing back and taking only the lesson with you. Think about how much time you have wasted in the past focusing on a loss. Is that how you want to move going forward?

It was a struggle to find time to commit to myself, and it didn't start with motherhood. Before I was a mom, I was already a daughter, a granddaughter, a sister, an employee, a business owner, a volunteer at church, and a student. My plate was full! How do you do anything for yourself with so much going on? I had to be intentional and strategic about what I wanted to do. I started telling people "no" a lot more often instead of always being available to help with everything. I started to prioritize my needs over other people and theirs. People aren't going to be happy about that and you may even feel some guilt but know that you are doing the right thing.

Being everyone's extra set of hands is a lot. Sure, they sing your praises. People love and appreciate you and that feels good. However, in reality, the people in my life who matter are going to love me regardless. So, I don't have to always be everything to everyone to receive love. It's ok to say that you can't do something or at least not that day. Everyone's emergency can't become your emergency. If you've been this person to everyone, the transition will be rough, but it's necessary.

I don't have
to always
be everything
to everyone
to receive
love.

Those who matter will understand. Those who don't understand, would have likely hindered you from what you need to do for yourself. It's ok to let them go.

I had to carve out uninterrupted time to do me. That could mean learning something new, going to the movies alone, reading a good book, praying, whatever I wanted to do. During that time, I also mapped out my goals and ideas and started to create plans for each of them. These things were only important to me. This was my stuff, and nothing was going to get in the way of me doing this. Trust and believe, the people pulling on you take time for themselves and will shut you out in a heartbeat. You know you call them sometimes and they don't pick up.

Constant growth requires consistency. If you consistently take time to work on you, the things that you enjoy, and the areas that you want to develop, you will see change and be happy with the results. If you are less committed and don't do this as much, your results will reflect that too. So, move things out of the way and get it in! You owe it to yourself to grow and to not sit on the sidelines watching people live like a movie. Let people watch you, especially those who secretly wish you would fail. Give them a front row seat! My Bible says that *"the Lord will prepare a table for me in the presence of my enemies."* Psalm 23:5 (New King James Version). That sounds like a front row seat to me.

On the other side of making the decision to put some focus on yourself, is empowerment and life elevation. There is major satisfaction in being able to sit back and enjoy the fact that you've accomplished something on your list. When you get there, reward yourself. You deserve it! Then continue to commit to yourself and work on the next thing. Before you know it, you would have positioned yourself to walk into something completely new and exciting for your life. You may look back and not even recognize the old you.

Key Connections

It's a hard realization, but once you start making new commitments to yourself and following through with them, not everyone will be happy about it or make the adjustment with you. Some people, even the people who may be special to you, are not going to hang in there with you. You must keep going. It doesn't have to mean that they're bad for you, jealous, or don't want to see you win. It could just be that you outgrew them. Unfortunately, a changed mind produces other changes that we don't always anticipate. Sometimes that includes changes in relationships. It can be sad, but it is something that you will have to be ok with.

I have been blessed to have good people in my life that genuinely love me. Even some of them are not meant to be around forever. I think that people come and go in and out of our lives because they are only meant to be with us for a season and I am ok with that. Meeting new people has created opportunities for me and allowed me to support others for a season as well. I think we need these experiences to advance to new levels in life. People also leave because their lives are changing and shifting. People get married, have children, move out of state etc. Sometimes, you're not meant to go where they're going. It works both ways.

Thinking back on the relationships that I've had over the years and where they are now is bittersweet. There was a time when we had a singles ministry at church, and we were all very close. We did a lot of things together, including praying and doing the work of the ministry. We also did things like bowling and skating etc. Then people started pairing off and getting married. Some moved. Others went to different churches. Now, I hardly speak to any of those people. A lot of them have moved on with their lives and are doing their thing. A few, I speak to on a regular basis because we had a closer connection. I think it was meant to be that way and it's ok.

When forming new connections, it's important to seek people who are connected to your vision. In fact, sometimes, you don't even have to seek them out. God will place people in your life who are meant to be there. Embrace it and take full advantage of having those connections. Learn how to learn from other people. So many of us are so accustomed to working out everything on our own as black women, especially those of us who are single, that we don't know how to glean from someone. We think we have to always have and be the answer because society made us feel that way.

I know that I have personally missed out on some learning opportunities because I did not have the right posture and was not in a place to receive. Now, I make it a point to think about what I can learn from each of my connections and how I can add to them as well. I am always positioning myself to have a reciprocal relationship where we are both learning and sharing. This is my "everybody wins" stance. It sets me up to have successful relationships with everyone that I meet, that I can always leverage when needed.

Is everybody winning in your relationships? This only happens with intent. This is not an accidental antidote. You must be intentional about establishing this with people. You shouldn't be the one always giving, nor the one always taking or receiving. As I mentioned in my book *"To My Girls"*, there are times when people are placed in our lives for us to pour into them and they may not have anything to give back. There may also be times when you are the person who needs pouring into with nothing to give. However, that shouldn't be the case in all your relationships. If it is, you need to take a look at yourself and why you are attracting or attracted to this type of situation.

Self-evaluation is always good and should include a look at who we allow into our space and how they contribute to who we want to be. If you do this regularly, you'll sometimes be surprised at what you learn about yourself and others. What's important is that after we take inventory, we put some action behind it and start making the necessary changes. Remember, change doesn't always feel good, but I guarantee that the right changes will feel good once implemented.

My core people are still in my corner, and I am still in theirs. I don't see that changing. The frequency in which we communicate changes from time to time with life changes, but we still know where we stand with each other. That's just a part of life and how things work. I often hear women say that it is hard to meet new friends as an adult. There is some truth to that. It's definitely not as easy as it was when we were kids. As children, we could be best friends just because we both had on a yellow shirt that day. Adult relationships are a little more complicated. Be open when God sends people into your life that you have a genuine connection with. It can seem rare.

Most of us, at some point or another, have been wronged by someone who we thought was a friend. That can create such a wall. This wall will hinder you from making valuable connections with the right people if you allow it. It makes you unapproachable. You have to learn to be friendly again, to trust again and to let things flow naturally without being fearful of being hurt. Trust God to guard your heart. Other black women are not your enemy. Other women in general are not your enemy.

Put yourself in situations to meet new people. They aren't going to break into your house to "Netflix and Chill" with you. Go outside! When you get ready to venture out, leave your superwoman cape at home. Black women carry so many labels. Let's not feed into them. We don't have a chip on our shoulders, we don't have too much masculine energy, we aren't aggressive, and we can get along. How you see yourself is how you will see every black woman that you encounter. Remove these labels from you first. Then you can remove them from everyone else in your own mind.

One of the things that I enjoy doing is attending events where I know I will be able to interact with like-minded people. I learn about these events sometimes through social media, or other friends. I also go straight to event sites and type in the kind of event that I am looking for. My search might include business strategy groups and mixers or single black women entrepreneurs. Lately, I've been interested in groups for black mothers. While attending these in-person events, I work the room. I smile and greet everyone and introduce myself. It's really that simple.

I genuinely show interest in other people and what they do. People love to talk about themselves and will spend hours doing so if you let them. During this process, when I hear something connected to something that I have going on, I discuss it and see what their mindset is on the topic. If it's in alignment, I've made a connection. If it's not, I enjoy the conversation and move on. You're not getting married that day. You don't have to commit to anything. Just talk to people. Best case scenario is that you'll meet a new friend.

It can be intimidating to put yourself out there, especially with people who you view as "more successful" than yourself, but these are the types of friends that we all need. You need to know people who can open doors for you and be prepared to walk through them when they do! I never want to be the smartest person in the room. I just want to keep up and learn. If everyone in the crowd is doing better than I am, I want to be in that room. This takes confidence, though. You can't step into these rooms being timid or feeling like you're less than someone else. You must own the room!

Confidence is attractive, especially to successful people. They are looking for those who can handle themselves in any environment and bring something to the table. Let who you are shine through. You belong in that space! There's a purpose in you being there! Your next level up might be in that room! You can thank me later, because I am confident that you will rock out with this and start making major waves in new circles. I trust that opportunity will be knocking, and you will be ready to answer. Stepping into new opportunities can be exciting and a little nerve wrecking, but you got this!

Chapter Two

Designing Your Own Life

Once we have gotten past what other people think and who is or is not going on the journey with us, it becomes time to design our lives. Our life design is based on God's plan and the desires that He places in our hearts. Cars, homes, and other material things are nice, but it's about a lot more than that too. How do you want to live? What is included in your design of your life? The answer to this question is going to be different for everyone and there is no right or wrong answer. The important thing is that you know the answer. I was surprised at how many people couldn't verbalize an answer to this question.

I always knew that working full time for someone else was not a part of my life design. As a result, I was always looking for a way out of that. From the earliest age, I remember thinking of ways to make money as an entrepreneur. I knew in middle school that I wanted to be a business owner. I wasn't sure exactly what I wanted to do, but I knew then that it didn't include going to work every day for someone else. Even though I have worked full time in the past, I never lost sight of this goal. Today, I can say that I haven't had a full-time job in eleven years. Again, you can have what you say.

I am not saying that going to work for someone is a bad thing. If you have a job, thank God for it. Entrepreneurship is not for everyone. Plus, I firmly believe that as Christians, we need to be in all fields using our God given talents and abilities to meet the needs of the people. Our plans are not the same and one is not better than the other, in general. This is why I always stress the importance of following your own path regardless of feelings of uncertainty or fear that try to creep in.

Many entrepreneurs will both work in their business and work a job because it's necessary to make their ends meet or it's simply a good strategy for retirement planning. Nobody knows what's best for you, but you. Make decisions based on that. I am currently back in school studying epidemiology in response to this recent pandemic. So, I will be working in the field contributing my new skills. Christians are definitely needed in the workforce. Go where God leads. Will I work forty long hours every week? It's unlikely, but I will be adding my supply to the profession.

Be so confident in your own purpose that being aware of what others are doing doesn't distract you. This is the biggest mistake that you can make, and it will without a doubt slow your progression. You have to be willing to go against the crowd and the norms and do what's right for you. There will be times when you will feel like you may be going in the wrong direction, because the path can be lonely, and your loved ones may not agree with you. In those moments, seek God. My mother has been telling me for years to get a job. Now, I just laugh because it's hilarious. I understand that generations before me think differently based on the times in which they grew up.

When you were a child, what did you see yourself doing in your future? I don't mean when you were five and wanted to be a superhero. I'm talking about as you grew a little older and started to have real aspirations. I wanted to be a teacher. I knew that very early on and went on to become a teacher. I worked with children for twenty years before going into entrepreneurship, though it was always the plan. I had a purpose in the education field to fulfill first. I came to understand that as life unfolded, and I grew in my walk with God.

Does the fact that I am doing something different now mean that teaching was not the plan for me? No, it doesn't mean that. It was the plan for that phase of my life. It wasn't a waste of time. The time that I spent as an educator, family support worker and education manager, prepared me for parenthood in so many ways and I got to meet some amazing children who are now thriving young adults. Every part of our journey fits together and

Be so confident in your own purpose that being aware of what others are doing doesn't distract you.

has purpose. I didn't know the purpose at the time. I just knew that I enjoyed teaching and working with children. It was and still is my passion.

Teaching is where I developed patience and an understanding of how children grow and develop. To this day, I use skills learned as a teacher. I just use them at home with my own children and sometimes in coaching adults too. Teaching gave me an understanding of my children's special needs and helped me to know how to meet them where they are. Now, as a homeschool parent, I am really leaning into my role as a teacher. So, overall, that phase in my life was super beneficial. I would have a whole other set of struggles without it.

Think about all the different things that you have done over the years and how you picked up skills along the way that currently support your professional journey. All things really do work together. In addition to skills, you have likely also grown as a person. I say all of that to say, embrace where you are. It is meaningful to your journey. You may not feel like you are living the life that you designed, but you may just be in the preparation stage. This is a necessary step to ensure that when you get where you want to be you don't mess it up. You'll be ready for it. So often we ask for things that we aren't truly ready to receive. Then we get mad when God doesn't present it to us on a silver platter at the time that we ask for it. There's a reason for that. You're still in preparation for it.

As you are designing your life and creating a plan to make things happen, be patient with yourself. We are our own biggest critic sometimes. Nothing just happens overnight because we want it to. I believe that God does things suddenly. I also know that this is not always how things unfold. Sometimes, you must put in the work over a period of time. Do not deceive yourself into thinking that all you have to do is pray and nothing will be required of you. At the very least, you'll have to believe and put action behind those prayers. You can't always just pray and walk away.

Acknowledge your accomplishments along the way. It's the biggest motivator. The fastest way to crush a dream is to not break it down into accomplishable steps. It will leave you feeling defeated and unsatisfied. Knocking things off your list and moving on to the next phase will make you feel like you're on your way. Be realistic with your goals. What can you accomplish in a week, a month, a year, etc.? Think about your current goals and decide on the steps that you will take to reach them. Give those steps deadline dates and try to stick to them. As you start marking the steps as accomplished, you'll be closer and closer to your big goal.

I am a fan of vision boards. I talk about vision boards in all my books and at every speaking engagement. I love the idea of putting a visual before my face daily of what I want to attract to my life. For me, it makes it real. It gives me a daily focus. I use my vision boards as a working document. I write on it as I accomplish steps and sometimes attach journal entries. It has become an interactive tool used to get me from point A to point B. If you made a vision board that has just become pretty pictures to look at, is it really your vision? It may be time to do another one, and this time be intentional about it.

Another strategy that I use is journaling. I like this strategy because it allows me space to write down the vision and how I plan to reach my goals. I also document how I feel about the process along the way. It's great to be able to look back on it and remember all the steps, feelings, emotions, challenges, and triumphs. It's good motivation for when I start working on the next goal. Write in your journal and read it. Don't forget that step. Simply writing is not enough. You'll forget what you wrote before you even put your pen down.

A common mistake with journaling, in addition to not being intentional, is not being consistent. Just writing things down randomly isn't going to work for you the way that you want it to. Decide if you want to add entries daily, weekly, or monthly and stick to your schedule. My suggestion is to have multiple journals for the various areas of your life that you want to use this strategy for. You can have journals for your business, home life, things that you're working on with your children, or whatever else you plan to document.

Set time aside to write in your journals and specify what you want to reflect on each time. I like to document wins, challenges, and what I plan to do next. Then I write my thoughts and feelings about the process. Sometimes, that part is nice and encouraging and sometimes it's frustrating and angry. It's all ok! Don't write in your journal as if you are writing to an audience and have to sugarcoat things. This is something that is only for you. Your feelings are yours and it's all a part of your journey. Nobody else will see it unless you share it.

Whichever strategy you use, either one that I've suggested or one that you find someplace else, be committed to it. It's important. It's valuable. It's going to get you to the next phase. Don't waste another day just going through the motions. Wake up daily with a purpose and a plan for that day. Take things one day at a time, but also plan. Prepare yourself for what you want to attract to your life and what you are asking God for. When you get it in your hands, girl, you're on fire! I remember someone commented on social media that they did not plan long term goals. She thought she was clowning me for thinking so far ahead. How sad it must be to not have a vision for your life. I always have set goals, and they always lead to something much bigger in the future.

This young lady thought that she was making me look silly, but she was really highlighting her own insecurities about her future. The crazy part is, I think she's amazing and very gifted. I also think that she is dealing with a level of fear that stops her from thinking ahead. Fear can jump on anybody. You can have it going on and still, deep down, be fearful. Other people may think you're great, but you have to know it and you have to use your own faith to manifest your greatness. That is a perfect example of how opinions don't matter, good or bad. It's all in how you see yourself.

Those Plans Can Change, Sis

What happens when you've planned it all out and it doesn't happen according to that plan? This is something that I know all about! My life is very different from what I thought it would be. At the time that I am writing this book, I am in my mid- forties, unmarried, with two children. That was definitely not the original plan! However, I am so thankful to God for where I am in my life. I am living my prayers! I know you think I'm crazy for praying for this, but it's not your plan. It's mine and it's not even my complete plan. This thing is not over and I am very comfortable ignoring opinions about my life and how God chose to unfold it.

I thought that by the time I was twenty-five I would be married and working on baby number three, four, or five. Yes, I wanted five children and a baby daddy who I shared a last name with. Well, it didn't work that way. I ended the ten plus year relationship with the love of my life at the age of twenty-five. We started real young. We did not have children together. He and I went back and forth in and out of relationship for the next five years after the breakup, and just never could get it together. So, I left the situation in search of God's plan because that wasn't it. I still think he's awesome. He's just not my dude.

Soon, I found myself over thirty, still without a husband or children and resenting the fact that I had wasted all those years with him. I really wanted to be a mother. I had spent years taking care of other people's children and wanted that for myself. So, I went to my Pastors with a plan that I wanted to share. I am laughing as I am typing this because I remember the conversation and their faces as if it were yesterday. I came to tell them that I was going to have artificial insemination, or that I was just going to have a baby with my ex, knowing that we were not ever going to be an ideal family living in the same household.

They didn't exactly think those were good plans for me. They love my ex but didn't love the up and down relationship and weren't really feeling artificial insemination all that much either. It's beautiful when someone knows you well enough to help you make a decision and it's one that you know is best for you. At some point in the conversation, I decided that I was going to chill for a few more years and see where God would lead me. That was a plan that they were on board with. We also discussed adoption and how there were so many children who needed good homes and people to love them. I put that option in my back pocket. I had always wanted to adopt children, but I wanted to do that after having a few biological children.

I don't know why I thought having another emotional attachment to my ex, in the form of a whole little person, would have been a good idea. I trusted him. I knew he would be a good dad, but no way was this plan going to be healthy for any of us. Though our judgement can get cloudy sometimes, it's never too late to create an alternative ending. I'm blessed to have chosen something different. I still trust him and still think he's a great dad to his son, but this plan was not it. Don't beat yourself up over your bad ideas, or even your bad actions. Move on from them.

For the next couple years, I focused on other areas of my life. I picked up new skills, grew my business, and did a lot of self-care during this time. It was a time of self-development. It was also a time of reflection about what I really wanted for myself. I didn't think about having children much during this time because my mind was occupied. I was just being good to me. Without knowing it, I was preparing myself to be responsible for another person's life. I needed that time to create a life that I could bring a child into. I couldn't bring children into a mess. They certainly weren't going to fix my mess like some of y'all think children do.

Right before the pandemic of 2020, I moved into a different house and then had a lot more space to utilize

Though our judgement can get cloudy sometimes, it's never too late to create an alternative ending.

and started to consider adoption. I contacted several agencies and quickly realized that these people were basically selling babies. There is no way that adoptions can legitimately range in cost from thirty to sixty thousand dollars. After deciding to not give these people every dime that I had, I decided to contact the local social services agencies to adopt through foster care. It was where the most need was and it was free. The only catch was that it was not likely that I would adopt a baby. Most children in foster care are older. I was ok with that.

When I say that this was God's plan, believe me! It became so obvious in the way that things just lined up so perfectly. A social worker came to my home to discuss the process and to check the home environment. As she was leaving, she received a text message that an adoption had fallen through. She shared her disappointment with me and left. Had she received that text just a minute later, I would not have even known about the situation. She just happened to be still in my doorway when the text came through. The children of this failed adoption are now my two beautiful children because that was God's plan. Even when it is His plan, it can still be quite the journey. Nobody said it would be easy.

Over the next few months, I checked in with her to ask if the girls had been adopted. I really didn't know anything about them because she couldn't tell me much due to confidentiality rules, and I wasn't yet eligible to adopt. My home study was not complete and I was not licensed at the time. However, for some reason, I had to know what was happening with them. So, I asked often. To make a super long story short, she waited for me. This social worker and the agency waited about six months for me to become eligible to adopt. Meanwhile, there were other families, who were ready and wanted these children. They put the whole process on hold until I was ready. Sign number two that this was God's plan. Are you keeping up?

As you go through your journey, God will show you that you are on the right track. You won't have to guess, but you will have to trust. I had to trust God this whole time that I was going to be the mother of these children. I had to set aside any fear that it would go any other way. During this process, that trust was tested a couple times. The good news is, I passed! I have the pictures to prove it. I am a "girl mom" and loving it! We are living proof that nothing can stand in the way of His plan, not even two parent households competing with your single self for an adoption.

Once I had been officially licensed and eligible, the fight began! There were six families that also wanted to adopt my girls. I continued to pray "Lord Your Will be done". I already loved these children whom I had never met. I loved them so much that I told God that if they were not meant to be my children, let them go to a family who would love them. In my heart, I knew they were mine. I just wanted to cover all bases and make sure that my heart was in the right place and that my intentions were not selfish. I wanted them more than anything in the world, but I also wanted them to have God's plan for their lives.

God again confirmed that these were my children. I know He was shaking His head. Like, how many times do I have to tell this girl? I started to get real serious about praying away the competition. One by one families were dropping out or being disqualified in one way or another. Then it came down to just me and one other family. I was questioning why they would choose me over a married couple. They could give these children an ideal two parent household. They weren't going to choose me! In those moments, I had to remind myself what God said.

It came time for my interview. I had to meet with about five social workers and supervisors. This was their opportunity to learn more about me and to see if I was a good fit for the children. Following the interview, I immediately contacted the social worker that I had grown familiar with to ask how she thought it went. I will never forget her words. She stated that the team still had to interview the other family because that's just how it works, but that I had already been chosen to be the children's mom. The team loved me and knew that I was the right one to love the children! One of the things that stood out to them was my background in education and working with children with special needs. Remember I told you that my time as a teacher was a part of the plan for my life? God will order your steps!

Fearless black woman, it doesn't matter what it looks like, God can do anything that He wants and if it's in His plan for you, it's going to come to fruition. You can have all types of odds stacked against you. None of that matters. You have to boldly take what God says belongs to you. Those children were mine before they were formed in their biological mom's womb. God was not taken by surprise when she proved to be unable to care for them. He already had a plan for them! I was always their mother! I just had to position myself and embrace that this was how I would become a mother.

I was about to step into God's plan for not only me, but His plan for my little girls too. I met them for the first time on my 40th birthday. What a birthday gift! I had instantly transitioned to having no children at all to being a mother of two. The two people who flipped my life upside down and brought so much joy and chaos that I didn't know if I were coming or going for a little while. If you're a mom, you know just what I'm talking about. Every day presents a new joy, a new challenge, and a new need for a long bath with some candles burning, headphones, and a locked door. My house is still chaotic, but I love it all.

Nobody Said It Would Be Easy

The biggest myth that we can tell ourselves is that the road is going to be easy. It won't always be! The question is, is it worth it? It's when you come face to face with this question that you take a long hard look at what you really want for yourself. You have to decide if you are willing to put in the work necessary to obtain and maintain the thing that you have been praying for. Sometimes we want things, but don't want to do what it takes to have or keep those things. Sometimes once you have it, there's no turning back or quitting. You have to figure out your next steps. That is especially true when it comes to parenting.

When I adopted my children, it was something that I really wanted and was committed to. I was all in from day one. Then I brought them home and life started happening. My family situation and home life was not ideal. My children were adjusting and so was I. They did a lot of testing during the first few months, and it was rough. I had to stand on the fact that this was God's plan, and it would be ok. Even though things were absolutely crazy then, I knew that this was right. It never felt wrong to me, even in the most stressful moments. I've never really had a problem sticking with something when I knew it was in God's plan for my life. This was the proving ground.

I wasn't prepared for all the stress of parenting. Our adjustment period wasn't cute. Caring for two children with a lot of needs weighed heavily on me at that time. I had help from my mom, but she went home every day. Then, I was on my own. One thing I learned is that your biggest challenge will become your greatest reward. We got through the rough times and created a strong bond. I would do it all over again if I had to. Today, my children are just your everyday happy, healthy children and I thank God for it. Everything isn't perfect, but whose situation is. I do know that we are perfectly right where we are meant to be.

Your situation can change just as drastically as mine did. You just have to stick with it and not give up because it's hard. Life is hard, but you have help. You also have the courage to meet challenges head on. You're fearless! You trust God! You know that it will all work out and God will get the glory! He is never going to lead you someplace and just walk away. I'm so happy that God is a hand holder. In this world all we hear is "The only person you can depend on is yourself" Well, that's not true for us.

What's your strategy for dealing with challenges? Please don't tell me that you ignore them like they will just go away. Having a plan for how you're going to face a challenge will help you to get ahead of it. Don't wait until things happen and catch you off guard. Some people will tell you that planning for a mishap is operating outside of faith. Well, I say that's crazy. You wear seatbelts in case something happens on the road. You have homeowners' insurance in case something goes wrong in your home. Plan a strategy for roadblocks that will try to come between you and your destination.

Knowing what you will do if you need to adjust your plan is not going against your faith. It's using the brain that God gave you. For instance, when I was planning my business, I proposed a coaching strategy. I also knew how I could change that strategy if it didn't catch. I had a marketing plan. In that plan, I had multiple strategies in case one didn't work. I have strategies for correcting my children. When one doesn't work or stops working, I have another plan in place. I am always prepared! Preparation and faith can exist together. It's unbelief that can't exist with faith.

A part of preparation is organization. It's hard trying to be prepared when you aren't first organized. Stop trying to operate without having both in place. You're fighting an uphill battle with this one if you are. Take time this week to organize your life and watch how much more smoothly things start going. You'll think more clearly, and your actions will be more in alignment with your goals. If you can master organization, preparation, and being intentional, you are doing big things!

I'm sorry that I can't tell you that life is easy, you won't have any challenges, and you don't have to be strategic about almost everything. You do. The good news is that once these things become your habits, it becomes easier, and you just flow with it. You will start to not even notice that you're doing it. It will just be what you do. You'll be smooth sailing and getting over the bumps in the road like a champ! So, do not be discouraged. Be empowered and take the necessary steps to get it all together.

People will tell you "It don't take all that." Those same people are likely not where they want to be, or they are, and they got there by doing all of this. They just don't want you to be there too. Yes, we all know people like that. It's sad, but true. That's why one of the first things I told you was to stay on your own path and ignore what everyone else is saying and doing. The people who secretly want you to fail are watching and waiting. When you're not failing fast enough for them, they will insert themselves into your life with bad advice. So, be careful who you let counsel you. Not everybody is your friend and not everyone wants good things for you.

The great news is that God can weed out these people. I once heard someone say "You don't need to trust people. You just need to trust God and love people". He will work it all out no matter what other people do to you. So, we don't have to walk around fearful that people have bad intentions towards us. We can just live our peaceful lives, using wisdom and minding our business. Let God reveal who is for and against us and act accordingly. He will not let you down.

Chapter Three

The Trauma of it All

I get it. For some of you, it's easier said than done. You've been through some things that have made it harder for you to do all these wonderful things that I've made sound so easy. You were probably reading and saying to yourself, "But my situation is different. There's no way anyone expects this to apply to me." Yes, I do. I acknowledge that you may have more of a climb than someone else might. However, let me remind you that everyone has their own story and most of us were not raised with perfect parents. Some of the most successful people in the world have the worst story to tell. They just didn't let it hold them back. They turned it into something good and useful. How are you going to use your storm?

I am not at all saying what you've probably heard a million times, "Just get over it". Having this expectation is also unrealistic. People who typically say this have either not been through anything or they have, and it has made them so hard that they no longer feel. For you, there may be some work to do. You have to deal with whatever it is that happened to you so that you can leave it in the past. There are various levels of trauma, but it's all trauma. So, don't let anyone downplay your experiences and place an unrealistic requirement on you to move on without taking your time and doing the inner work. Only you know when you have healed and can come out on the other side of the mess.

Though there are many adults walking around still dealing with childhood trauma, it isn't always from childhood. Sometimes, it's a lot more recent. Personally, I've experienced both. I didn't realize that my experiences were traumatic in my life until recently. You may have hidden trauma too. It's important to uncover and process it. Do you have negative memories from your past that you often think back on? Pay attention to what is happening to your body when those things come to mind. Do you clench your teeth? Do you get teary eyed? How does it make you feel? Don't try to suppress those feelings. Feel what you feel.

I remember a lot of things that I don't want to. One memory that comes to mind more often than I would like is my father being on the porch crying because he couldn't come back into our house. There was a good reason for that and it did not involve my mother being spiteful or trying to keep us from him because of their personal issues. In fact, she never did that. She always wanted us to have a relationship and never said anything negative about my father in my presence. In that moment, she made the right decision considering the circumstances. I would have done the same thing as a mom if I were in her shoes. However, it was a traumatizing experience for me that I still think about to this day. As a child, I just wanted my daddy. As an adult, I understand it.

The expectation for black women to be strong is sometimes so prevalent that often we are not properly cared for. Our feelings are ignored. We're expected to just keep going no matter what. So, what do we do with our trauma? We sweep it under the rug and keep on keeping on. This is so unhealthy and unfair, but it is reality for a lot of us. I encourage you to speak up more often about how you feel. I believe that is one of the first steps in healing. Make people hear you and don't let the aggression stereotype silence you. Your feelings matter. You matter!

A recent experience that I am still dealing with is the car accident that ultimately caused my father's death and all the things that occurred in between. The accident occurred in January of 2022. It left him severely and irreversibly brain damaged. For ten months, I watched my father suffer and slip away. If you have not experienced that, trust me, you have no idea what it's like and I hope you never come to understand it for yourself.

The expectation for black women to be strong is sometimes so prevalent that often we are not properly cared for.

It's something I can't fully describe or explain. Getting through this took a lot of prayer and support.

It was a horrible ten months. There were so many ups and downs, concerns, worries, fear, let down, drama and sadness. There was also hope and faith. I hoped for the best outcome and had faith that whichever way that it turned out, God was in control and carrying us through it. Thinking back on it, I know I only survived it still in my right mind because of God and who He is to me. Still, it was the hardest thing that I've had to endure in my life. Obviously, my father passed away, but my prayer was still answered. I prayed that his suffering would end and that he would be healed. He was. There is no sickness or pain in Heaven.

Having faith does not mean that we don't have feelings and emotions. It doesn't make us immune to what's happening. It just helps us to get through it without being controlled by those feelings and emotions. We are not robots. Often, we are made to feel like as Christians we should be able to just pray and everything just goes away, carrying all the associated feelings with it. I haven't experienced that. If you have, write me a letter, and let me know what that's like. I have experienced God's peace in the midst of a storm, yes. The storm was still real, though. Don't feel bad for being human and having a human experience.

Watching my father wake up in a nightmare everyday was a nightmare for me. He couldn't talk, eat, walk, or anything. Everything had to be done for him. There were times when I wasn't even sure if he knew who I was. Can you imagine? To make matters worse, there was a lot of family drama that occurred during that time. I am still trying to wrap my mind around all that happened. Stressful situations really do bring out the worst in people. I understand that everyone was hurting and afraid. Still, there is no excuse for how things were handled by some people.

The silver lining in it all is that out of this traumatic experience, I became closer to some family members. I'm thankful for that. I really got to see who was riding with me, for real. As for some others, God is still working on me. The hurt hits different when it comes at the worst time in your life. The best advice that I can give when things like this occur is to allow yourself time to process everything. Even if it takes more time than you thought it would, it's ok. It's been over a year for me, and I am still processing.

To begin healing, I did something that I told my father I was going to do before the accident. I bought another house and moved my children to Maryland. I didn't want to raise them in the same city that they were adopted from. I wanted a new start for them someplace different. I also wanted better school options. I started looking for my house about a month after he had passed and within two months had made my purchase. With my cousin's help, I started small renovations to make my home how I wanted it to be. I'm still in that process. It's been a lot of work, but also fun and therapeutic. I am enjoying it.

There was talk about how I moved on quickly from grieving my father. People judged me, but they didn't know why I did it and I didn't care. It wasn't their business. The only thing that mattered is that I knew my father was proud of me. He always was. I remember how excited he would get any time I did anything. He was always cheering for me. I know that he still is. He knew I was going to live my dreams. He knew that there was fearlessness in me. In a lot of ways, I am a lot like he was. He was also a very bold person who didn't care what people thought. He was always willing to go his own way. He was also an entrepreneur in his own right and good at it.

I had already conquered fearlessly stepping into motherhood as a single woman, but this move made things different. I would no longer be walking distance from my mom's house, like I was in DC. Now, I had to do it without her daily active involvement. I was used to her being there every day helping with everything. Now, I would have to do it on my own. I knew it would be different for all of us but didn't discover the magnitude of this difference until the actual move. The reality check was real! It still is. 24/7 parenting on your own is a beast! Even though I am finding my footing, I'm still trying to get my mother to move into my house.

Being a mom and trying to juggle everything is a lot. The funny thing is that I can already see how God has planned to make something good come out of this experience of struggling by myself. When I adopted my children and settled into motherhood, I no longer had a desire to get married. I was happy just being a mom. In the past year since my move, I again have the desire to have a partner and a father for my children. I see the benefit in two people raising children together in the way that I had before. It's also very much what my children want. I hear this from them constantly. God, I definitely see what You're doing with this! I'm looking forward to our little family being complete.

My whole life is a testimony of how God has always had His hand on my life and everything concerning me. He is always working things out on my behalf in a way that will bring me the most successful outcome. When your mind and heart are open to God, He can change you in ways that benefit you, even when you don't yet see how. He will make it all work in your favor! The key is to be open and as I said before, follow instructions. That following instructions part is what gets a lot of us tripped up. We can ask for things and enjoy them when they come, but the in between part can be rough.

Get You Together First

Buying the house was the easy part. The other phase of my healing is what I am still working on. I'm working on repairing my heart. In your lifetime, you will be hurt by people, and you will also hurt people. Those are the facts. You may not do it intentionally. They may not do it intentionally. That doesn't make it hurt less. In this phase of my process, I had to stop looking at the people who hurt me and start looking at me. Taking accountability and examining where you are, and your role is an important step in moving on. Knowing that you did all that you could do in a situation helps with closure. If you didn't, knowing that creates space for you to make things right. You will either need to forgive or be forgiven after you think it through, most times both.

Forgiveness is more about you than them. We know that, right? You've heard this before. Forgiveness frees you. It allows you to move on. So, even if you don't want to forgive, you should. You should for yourself if for no other reason. That's a given. The other side of it is that to not forgive is to operate in fear. You fear that forgiving will allow the person to creep back in and hurt you again. You fear that forgiving will make you look weak. You may even fear that forgiving will make others feel it's ok to treat you poorly. None of this has to be true. Just let go of all of that. Deal with your fear and forgive for you.

Forgiveness doesn't mean that the person once again has access to you. You can forgive and still not open the door to them or their mess. Forgiveness doesn't mean to be friends or even acquaintances. Forgiveness doesn't require that. All you must do to forgive is release them for what they've done to you and settle it in your heart that it's over and will no longer play a role in how you feel. You may find it easier to forgive if you think about what made them do whatever they did to you. You may even feel sorry for them. Remember hurt people, hurt people. Knowing this helps you to better understand where their actions came from and reminds you that you don't want to be a hurt person who hurts others. Also remember that healed people can lead others to healing.

You want to be a healed person so that you can make an impact on this world that will never be forgotten. You want to walk in God's plan for your life. You can't do that while carrying a lot of pain. I used to always hear people say that black people don't go to therapy, we go to church. Nowadays, I don't hear that so much. It has become more common to hear people of color discussing therapy. I'm glad that this is becoming normalized. There is also value in taking your issues to the church. There should be a healthy balance where this is concerned. There is a reason why people go to school and have specialized skills in this area. We shouldn't feel like we have to chose therapy or faith.

When selecting a therapist, be sure to choose one that is a good fit for you. That might mean choosing someone who looks like you, or not. It could mean finding someone in your age category, or not. It's completely up to you and your preferences, but make it work for you. If you find it to not be working, don't be afraid to seek someone else. Keep trying until it starts working. It's vital that you stick with it until you've made progress. Many times, people start therapy and give up too soon or stop because it's uncomfortable. This will leave you right where you started.

Whatever you do, don't be weighed down by your past or even your present circumstances. Implement some type of coping strategies to get you through. Prayer works! That's my number one coping strategy. Discover the thing that works for you and practice it. Write some scriptures in your journal for various situations. Meditate on them. Quote them to yourself. Life can be a lot and it gets really rough if you have nothing to stand on. This goes along with what I was sharing earlier in the book about preparing for a mishap. Have those scriptures already written out and deep in your heart ready for when fear and unforgiveness starts to rise up.

Before you convince yourself that you can't do this or that it won't work, think about what you have to lose. The only thing that is going to leave you is drama and pain. You have nothing else to lose by giving it an honest try. You have everything to lose if you don't. Your peace will be gone. Your joy will be stolen. Your happiness will be surface level at best. I know you don't want to live like that. I know you want to be the best possible version of yourself and that is achievable. You owe it to yourself to be that chick!

What's Next for You?

Now, it's time to rebuild! Like everything else, what rebuilding looks like is unique to you. For you, rebuilding could mean to start focusing on your self-care routines. I don't know how people survive without ever getting a massage or a pedicure. It's so healthy for you. It relieves stress and releases toxins. Both are super necessary. I understand that these are expenses that you may not be able to afford monthly but work it in some kind of way. Make that happen for yourself. I believe you will feel better. It's a time to just relax and free your mind.

One thing that I highly recommend is a retreat of some sort. I am planning a rest retreat for my birthday this year and I can't wait! I plan to rest like I've never rested before. I am starting my retreat with some spa treatments, stretching, and healthy food. Followed by prayer and journaling. Lastly, I am going to sit in my room and be alone with my thoughts for the entire day, completely unplugged. Day two, I will spend eating well, relaxing in a jacuzzi, and soaking in a nice deep spa bathtub. I'm putting everyone on notice ahead of time not to call or text me for 48 whole hours. Then on the third day, I will head back to real life. Short, but sweet and necessary.

You may want to travel. Traveling can be so freeing. It is a great time to reflect and plan, especially if you travel solo. I know that is a huge step for a lot of people. It's something that I really enjoy. I use the time to set goals, write, pray, and just think without distractions. This may not be for you and that's ok. I know a lot of women who love it and an equal amount who do not. If traveling alone will cause more stress or anxiety, don't do it. Invite someone who you enjoy spending time with. Choose wisely! Otherwise, you could be creating a disaster.

I try to always travel with someone who has a similar travel style as I do. For example, I don't travel with people who will be looking for a party because I travel mostly to rest. So, my ideal travel partner just wants to lay by the water at the beach. We may enjoy a party environment at some point during the trip, but it's not a priority for either of us. The trip ends up being enjoyable for us both because we spent the time how we wanted to. I don't know about you, but I don't spend money, pack bags, and spend hours on a plane, to not enjoy myself. My plan is always to get the most out of my trips. Sometimes, that means being alone.

I also enjoy reading self-development books, studying the Bible, and listening to podcast about subjects that interest me. Reading opens my mind up to learning something new that I might need in my toolbox to use later. Podcasts do the same. By now you know that I am a journaling Queen. I like to record new things that I'm learning in addition to downloads from God. I keep one next to my bed. It captures all my thoughts as I navigate through daily life. I encourage you to journal. Trying to keep so many things in your head is unproductive.

All these activities can add to you, make you feel better, and train your mind to think about you sometimes. As you are learning and growing, you will likely seek more learning opportunities and more growth, and it will become your new habit. Continue to build yourself up until you are happy with who is staring back at you in the mirror. Be patient. This is not something that you can implement overnight, and your progress will take some time. This is especially true if you are looking for significant growth.

Healing and building are both a lot to wrap your mind around, I know. It probably seems like so much work, but hopefully, it also sounds like a fun and rewarding process. If it doesn't it's only because it's one that you aren't accustomed to and it feels uncomfortable. Do it anyway. Don't make an excuse for not working on you. It just takes a little courage. You picked up a book about living fearlessly. Do it! Think about what's waiting for you on the other side of

Continue to build yourself up until you are happy with who is staring back at you in the mirror.

whatever you are currently dealing with. Isn't it worth it to get to a new place in your life journey.

Don't mask your emotions for anyone, but don't live in them either. Feel what you feel and then navigate your way out of that space. The longer you sit there, the harder it will become to move away from it. I had to learn a long time ago to drop things before they drop me. Strong emotions that you allow to fester will bring you to your knees eventually. Somebody reading this knows exactly what I'm talking about. You've probably been there and done that and have the t-shirt to prove it! Practice letting negativity go quickly.

Focus on the people and things that are good for you. Invest your time there. Put your heart into those things and those people. Focusing on negativity only brings more negativity. When you give your attention to good things, you attract more good into your life. We are always creating patterns. Our thoughts create actions and actions have outcomes. We recreate those same actions and outcomes repeatedly until our thought life changes. Yes, we are that powerful! We can create with our thoughts! Decide what you want to create.

Remember that whatever you create, you are also creating that for your children. No matter how hard you try to hide behind a fake smile, it will affect them in some way. You are only fooling yourself if you believe otherwise. They don't have the ability to sift through your mess. Our children feel all our energy and experience all our emotions. Be careful what you pass on to them. Be intentional about this for them. Most of your processes become theirs. Has anyone ever told you that your children act just like you or have you noticed that yourself? There you have it!

The Journey is Yours

You're never going to be the perfect parent or the perfect person. Don't put that pressure on yourself. Self-development is a lifelong journey. You'll never be finished no matter how far you've come. We should always be becoming better and forever on our way to something more than what we were or had the day before. The pressures of the world are fierce. We are expected to have it all, do it all and be it all. Don't give that expectation space to play around in your head.

I won't get into depression and other diagnosis that requires a professional in that field, but I will say that comparing your life to the life of someone else brings on negative emotions. Most people can find positive things to focus on in their own lives if they just stop making comparisons. Keep in mind that your journey is yours. It's never going to look like the journey of another person and nobody else will get your rewards or see the light meant for you at the end of your tunnel.

Many people get stuck in how things have always been and may even feel like they can never change. Maybe you don't have the tools to change things. However, you can always obtain them. In most cases, I believe it starts with a decision to be different. Once the decision has been made, things can start to line up. Decisions bring about actionable steps. Actionable steps bring about results. I know I said earlier that we can create and change things with our thoughts, but don't get it twisted. Nothing ever gets done or changes from thoughts alone. That's just the beginning.

My journey has led me down some paths that I did not see for myself when I planned my life. However, I was open to God's plan and I ended up where He wanted me to be and where I could experience His best for me. I am excited about what else is in the pipeline as I continue to be open and obedient. A key piece of advice that I can offer is to not look to others for direction. People can only give advice based on their perspective. God's plan for your life may be higher than they have ever seen, experienced or even thought. So, you can't trust people's opinions of your life in that way. Seek the Lord!

There were many times in life when I asked God, why me. Why did I have to have an absent father during my childhood? Why did I have to pay my own way through college? Why did I not get married at twenty-five? Why did I not have a high paying job? Why hasn't my business grown to millions yet? Why? Why? Why? I had to stop looking at things this way and trust that regardless of any hardship God has a plan for me and I will see it through. The why doesn't matter as much as the how. How am I going to come back from this stronger?

Many people say why me, but only some do something about it. It's a fearless action to do what your circumstances say that you can't do. It requires stepping out on faith and trust in the Lord. You're not fearful of failure or embarrassment. You just do your thing and believe God. What's the worst that can happen? Weigh that against the best that could happen. That's usually how I pick my battles. It has not let me down once. I win or I learn. Either way, I walk away better. The issue for a lot of people is that every time they don't win in the way that they thought they should, they feel defeated and never recognize what they learned and how it positioned them to be better and to win in the grand scheme of things.

Chapter Four

You Just Might Be a Catch!

I had to include a chapter on dating because it is hardly ever spoken about from the perspective of a single Christian woman. It's almost like the church thinks that we are supposed to just pray, and the man of our dreams will come knocking at the door and we will get married, no dating involved. That's not real life. In real life, we date to get to know men and to learn things about ourselves, just like everybody else does. Once you have put in the work and are operating in your fabulousness, you can put some effort into your dating life, if you so desire.

If you are one of the single women who has been convinced that you are not supposed to date different men, today you can come out from under that cloud. Don't let fear of how others view your dating life deter you from getting what you want. There is nothing wrong with going on dates. You have to meet multiple people to decide what you like and don't like. Your behavior during those dates is what can make it an issue, not going on the date. Dating does not equate to having sex. It is not the same thing. Dating is going out and having a good time with another human. Nothing more and nothing less.

So many Christian women believe that dating is wrong and appears promiscuous. That's craziness! I know I personally am happy that I did not marry the first person who looked at me twice. I have greatly benefitted from getting to know different people and what they bring to the table. It was through this process that I learned what I want for me. Had I married the first guy that I fell in love with at a young age, I would likely be unhappy today because I would have outgrown him in so many ways, and I would wonder what other people were like. I think that's normal. Not only is it normal, but it's perfectly ok as long as you are not married. Don't let the church Elders punk you into settling for the first saved person who smiles at you. Having a relationship with God does not necessarily make you compatible.

I am very fortunate to not belong to a church where people get this involved in my personal life and I have not been discouraged from dating, but I have heard the stories, and they amaze me. If you've been at a church your whole life, have great respect for the people whose leadership you are under, and they have influenced all your decisions, it will take a level of courage to step out and do what you feel is right for you. You can maintain love and respect for people without diminishing your ability to have your own relationship with God and decide for yourself what is appropriate.

You also do not have to go on group dates. Now, this is one that I have heard time and time again in the church. A group date can be fun and allows you to see how the person interacts with other people, but it is also important to see how they interact with just you. You need to be able to trust your grown self around a man without feeling like something is going to go down. You can go on a movie date and keep all your clothes on, right? If not, stay home. You're not ready to date if you need a babysitter. I know some women prefer group socialization. They don't know how to interact with men because they've always been taught that they shouldn't.

I was surprised to learn that some adult women are afraid to date. Like, literally nervous around men. I can't relate. I love men and everything that they bring to the table. I am here for it! I remember going out with a girlfriend to a popular restaurant that doubled as a major hang out spot on the weekends. As we were sitting at the table and ordering food, I noticed a guy staring at her. I tapped her and let her know. "Hey, that guy has been staring at you for a while. I think he may come over here." She was horrified! I was baffled! I am sitting at the table looking at this forty-five-year-old woman about to cry because a man was looking at her. She was visibly bothered. I couldn't believe it! I still can't believe it to this day!

I am not at all saying that you should entertain any and everyone who is interested. Let's not confuse what I'm saying. There have been plenty of times that I have run in the other direction when certain guys approach me. There are a lot of lame dudes out there and even more that just don't align with who I am and my beliefs. For me, that's not someone whom I would allow to pursue me. It would be a waste of his time. You can be selective and apply whatever selection rules you want.

I know that for some people beliefs and religion are not an issue. I am not one of those people. I am not interested in dating someone who I don't have that in common with, for a lot of reasons. That is a personal decision that I think only you and God can work through. Personally, I'd rather be single than date someone who believes differently from me. I just think that it opens a door to too many complications and a lot of confusion. For example, I have come across men who don't celebrate holidays because of either their religious beliefs or personal choices. Well, holidays are important to me. I celebrate big! I celebrate everything! When I have a life partner, I would want him with me for these celebrations right along with all my other loved ones.

Some might call that petty. However, I disagree. Having what you want is not petty. Not wanting to compromise on things important to you is not petty.

You don't have to work through anything with anyone who is not your husband. In the dating phase, you can walk away from whoever you want to for whatever reason you want to. Don't let someone convince you that you have to accept anything less than what you want. I have heard a million times that there is a shortage of good black men, and I should basically just pick one and settle down. I have not allowed that opinion to dictate how I do life and who I do life with.

It's also important to remember that nobody is perfect. So, you might meet someone who is a good match for you but doesn't check all your boxes. If it's not a major lifestyle compromise involved, maybe you give it a shot. That person could be just what you need. Dating is a process that should be fun. Getting to know people should be enjoyable. Don't apply all of life pressures to it. Keep things light and exciting with no expectations until expectations have been spoken and agreed upon. I personally would let him initiate that, but that's just me. He should be able to state where he wants things with you to go. If you lead that conversation, you'll be leading everything and will be tired by month three.

Let things happen naturally. Don't be out here asking dudes after a month if they are going to marry you. Instead ask other questions that will help you get to know him as a person and his intentions. Learn as much as you can, so that you can make an informed decision about him. Don't forget to ask God too. Sometimes, we

Not wanting to compromise on things important to you is not petty.

get so caught up and haven't asked God anything. Then we wonder why things didn't work out and we ended up with our feelings hurt. I know it's not just me. Y'all have done this too.

Be Smart, Not Fearful

If you desire to be married, you have to let go of the fear of being hurt. You can guard your heart without pushing everyone away from it. Don't go into anything giving everything right at the beginning but give someone a chance to be the one. Just go into it with your eyes wide open, use your brain and don't get caught up in it too quickly. You'll be fine if you listen to the voice of God and seek His direction on which way to go with people. I will drop a dude quick and move on just as quickly. I have no reason to deal with anybody's red flags. I am single and free, and I'm a great catch!

I have had some dating experiences that were crazy! I could write a book about that alone. Trust me, if you like drama, that would be your favorite book. A guy that I dated recently was a fast talker and nothing that he said sounded true. I called him out on that when we first met and stopped talking to him because of it. After a couple weeks, he contacted me with a business opportunity. I knew that he was successful in business and very well connected. He used this as the doorway back in because he knew it would be the only way that I would talk to him again. I still should have said no and walked away.

This man tried to destroy me spiritually and emotionally. That's how I knew he was sent from hell. He was the devil! I have never in my life met a person more narcissistic than him. The thing is, I was mentally and spiritually stronger than he was. So, his plan failed, but not for lack of trying. He really tried to get me. I might not always make the right decisions the first time, but one thing I am not, is crazy! I ran from him so fast, business opportunity and all. Nothing can hold me where I don't want be. I will leave money on the table every time if it means I leave with my peace.

I didn't have this experience because I was dating. I had this experience because I wasn't listening to the Holy Spirit on the inside of me telling me to not entertain him. My goal in sharing my embarrassing mistake is for you to see what happens when you're not obedient and do what you want to when God is saying no. You have experiences like mine. I also want you to understand that dating is not the problem. I could have easily avoided the situation. I made a choice. Now, I choose to be far more selective. I thought I was being selective then. I just wasn't selecting based on the right criteria.

I've also had a lot of really positive experiences with people that just turned out to not be a match for me for one reason or another. However, those people taught me what I like and don't like in a partner. So, today I am very clear about what I want beyond simply knowing that I want him to be Christian. There are a lot of Christian men whom I have zero interest in and won't likely ever. That's ok. Christianity may be a factor in my choosing, but there is a lot more that needs to be in place for me to want to date him.

Fear can cause you to have a very unattractive chip on your shoulder. It will turn people away from you, especially a man who is interested in a wife. I have never met a man who didn't want a partner to be soft and peaceful. The problem is, some of them didn't know that they were the reason why some women are not that way. Still, you can't expect "the one" to accept that or work his whole life to chip away at your past experiences. It's not fair. This goes back to what I shared in previous chapters about working on you first. Nobody wants to pay for another man's wrongdoing. You have the responsibility of creating your own happiness. That starts with working out your issues and allowing happiness in.

Make sure you are happy and whole before you attempt to date. That's the only way to bring happiness and wholeness to another person. Would you accept you the way that you are today? If the answer is no, you can't make someone else accept it either. I know that there are men who will deal with anything you dish out. Personally, he wouldn't be my type. If that's your thing, go for it. However, the issues on the inside of you still have to be dealt with so that you can accept yourself. Just because someone allows you to be a certain way, doesn't mean you should stay that way. Eventually, they will grow tired of you once you have drained all the life out of them.

Enjoy Your Single Life!

You should enjoy every moment and every phase of your life, including singleness. It has many benefits that you may be surprised are hard to let go of. For me, I know it's going to be sharing my bed, closet, and bathroom. I have been single for a long time, my whole life. I have not had to share this type of space with anyone since childhood. I am not looking forward to this, but I hope that once I fall in love and decide to commit my life to someone that I won't mind as much. Even still, I know it will be quite the transition. I like laying all over my whole bed. I also like leaving stuff all over my bathroom countertop without someone else complaining about it. My closet is jammed packed, and I have no plan to stop buying stuff and packing it in. These are things that I will have to adjust in marriage for sure.

Another thing that I enjoy about being single is doing whatever I want to without considering how someone else may feel about it. I just decide what I am going to do and go do it. The only considerations I need to give is to my children and they are not decision makers. In marriage, there is a lot of compromise and team decision making. That's not really my jam, but I'll cross that bridge when I get there. At least I know that this will be the case and I am not going into it blindly. I am also not going into it unwillingly. I'm just going to enjoy this phase of doing what I want to all the time, until it is no longer the phase that I am in.

Getting to a place of recognizing the sacrifices involved in marriage took time. As a younger person, I just wanted to be married. I didn't think about the work that was involved. It was just a fun thing to do that would give me a best friend for life and cut my bills in half. As I grew older and started to really understand what marriage is, I started to see that I was not ready for it. I am so thankful that I did not get married as a young person. Today, I am ready. However, I am in no rush. I appreciate where I am and enjoy it fully. I am sure that I will enjoy marriage also, at the appointed time.

Someone reading this has been married before and now find yourself single. You may struggle to find your groove in your new lifestyle. The best advice I can give you is to highlight the things about singleness that you enjoy instead of focusing on the parts that you don't or the fact that this was not the plan. Sometimes, singleness can be seen as a negative thing and all your experiences become negative only because you just can't see the good in it. Yes, you are used to being married, but was it a good marriage? Were you at peace? Can you be at peace now? Were you happy? Can you be happy now? Find the bright side.

Others may be single due to the death of a spouse. I can't begin to imagine your pain. I do understand how traumatizing death can be. Everyone grieves in their own way and should be allowed the time and space to do that. It may take you a long while to even consider yourself single. Just take life one day at a time and discover you along the way. You were dealt a bad hand, but you can still enjoy your life, which is what your spouse would have wanted for you. Go through your process. Everyday won't be great, but some will, and soon your good days will outweigh your bad ones.

No matter how you became single, you have to allow yourself to be ok with it at some point. I think this is especially true if you do want to get married for the first time or marry again. Being ok as a single person is one of the first signs of being ready to get married. The best partner for me is out living a full life and is happy with himself. I don't want to pair up with someone who has been just sitting around waiting for me to show up in his life. I want a man who has God as the source of his happiness. It may sound weird, but I want to come second in his life. God should always be first. I want to be a welcomed addition to his life, not his whole life. That's a lot of pressure.

No matter how you became single, you have to allow yourself to be ok with it at some point.

The Single Mom's Club

I have to mention this. Even though we think that people know this, some really don't. If they did, we wouldn't see so many stories of things going horribly wrong. Ladies, don't have a bunch of men around your children! Don't even have one man around your children that you have not properly vetted. This opens the door to the possibility for bad things to happen. Not only are your children impressionable and vulnerable, but they also have absolutely no way of protecting their own heart or bodies against an adult. Being a responsible parent is always putting your children's needs ahead of your own. You may desire and need a partner, but they need safety.

To this day, my children have seen me around one man. I dated him for seven months before he ever met them. Even then, they never saw him in my house. We all went to a park together and that was the extent of them meeting. He and I ended our relationship not long after. My children had seen him once, they had no attachment to him, and I was able to move on without them being involved. They couldn't care less. If I ask them now, I bet they don't even know his name and that's the way it should be until it's serious and secure. They were never at risk emotionally or physically.

I don't let my children listen to my phone conversations with men and I don't tell them when I am going on dates. I can't believe how some of y'all allow minor children to be in your business like that. My children need zero exposure to adult things. I am the gatekeeper. I control all information that reaches them. My dating life is not their business. Stop putting your children on the phone to say hi to people that they don't even know. It's really not cute and you're teaching them to be overly friendly with strangers. I know you don't mean to, but that is a form of grooming.

A guy whom I had been talking to for a few days did the weirdest thing and I never spoke to him again afterwards. He had been telling me that he has a daughter who lives with him. One night we were on the phone using Facetime, and he decided to prove this by going into her room while she was sleeping. He showed me his daughter sleeping in her bed. That bothered me to my core! It was absolutely ridiculous! What a violation of privacy. There is no way I could ever trust this man around my daughters. At the very least I knew that he would not protect them because he doesn't protect his own. What was the purpose in him doing that? What if she had been in her panties on top of the blanket? Just weird!

This is why I don't give access to my babies. For a man to be around them, especially in our home, he would have to be something special. I have not gotten to that point yet with anyone and I am in no rush to. Yes, it slows down my personal life. However, my mind is on what is most important. The right man will understand and be patient with me and we will be just fine. Until then, I will continue exactly as I have been.

How shameful would it be to give the wrong person too much access. I pray that you make good decisions regarding dating and children.

I know someone is thinking that the actions of that father were no big deal, but it was super inappropriate. What if she had been awake and understood that her father was basically bringing a stranger into her bedroom in the middle of the night. Yes, I was on the phone, but video chat placed me in her bedroom. It's all so yucky and makes my skin crawl. I would never violate my child like that. Our home is a private space, and they should always feel safe here, especially sleeping in their own beds. I also think about what things like that teach them. Will his child think that it's ok to have strange people around while you're in bed?

Another thing that I stand on is not allowing men to buy things for my children. That's a big no no. Before you allow your children to accept gifts from someone, know them well. Be comfortable with their intentions. Make sure he isn't doing so in order to gain their trust for the wrong reasons. Also, have conversations with your children about situations like this. You should be doing this frequently, not frequently enough to cause fear, but enough that it sinks in. You don't want your children to fear being around people, but you want them to be aware.

In addition to being diligent and putting your children first, pray over them daily. Thank God for protecting them. Also, pray over your husband. Ask God to send someone who will love and protect your children as his own. Ask for a father figure and a leader for them and your whole household. Even if they have an active father, your husband will be the one living with them. Be specific about what you want. You don't just want any man, right? You want the right man who is meant to enter your family and provide love and security.

As I said, I do believe in dating multiple people and the benefits of doing so, but I also understand that once you have done that, you are over it. You don't want to casually date for years and years. You want the end result of that process to be that "the one" finds you and you get married. You do get to a point where you don't want to date anymore. I am at that point. This doesn't mean that I am going to get married today. It just means that I am content where I am and have gotten what I needed to out of the dating process.

A friend of mine told me the most beautiful story recently. She's a minster and business owner and had just been living her life and serving. She had gotten tired of dating and told God that she didn't want to date anyone else. She was ready for her husband. Soon after, she met him and got married. They are truly a match made in Heaven. That's what I want for you and for me as well, a match that we know is from above. It will be such a beautiful thing and worth all that you learned on your way to meeting him. If you just exercise some patience, it will all work out.

What I want you to take away from this chapter the most is that the right person will come along. While you are waiting for him, dating, and enjoying life, remember that your children come first. They are your top priority. The man who is the one for you, will understand that you are not perfect. You have worked on preparing yourself for him but won't always get it all right. He won't either. He will also be patient regarding the fact that you can't just get up and go because you have children. He will understand that they are first in your life (until marriage). As a husband he will understand his role in your life and the lives of your children. Just take things one day at a time.

Chapter 5

The Best Version of You

Your personal and professional development are equally important to your overall life satisfaction and happiness. The world doesn't expect much from us as black women, regarding success. In fact, they seem surprised every time we win! However, God has equipped us to do all things. We can take what the world tried to dump on us and turn it into something great. We are bold, beautiful, intelligent, gifted, and then some. We can do anything that anyone else can do and, in many cases, we can do it better! It's time to stand tall and do just that. No more making ourselves small to appear less intimidating or being quiet so people won't label us aggressive or bossy. We are here and we are powerful.

I have watched so many women get passed over for things that they know they should have both personally and professionally because they passively sit on the sidelines of life. They allow people to step over them as they watch and convince themselves that they are ok with it. I realize that everyone does not have my personality. Not everyone is naturally assertive. However, you can assert yourself when necessary if you just decide to. For some people, you just have to get tired of things the way that they are and decide to create something different.

Being assertive does not mean to be rude or nasty to people. Neither does it mean to be obnoxious and overbearing. It simply means that you stand up and stand out for yourself. Make people recognize you. Stop fading into the background. Make it impossible for people to overlook you when it comes time for that promotion. Get the recognition that you deserve for a job well done. Be a leader, a trailblazer, a major contributor to the things that you are connected to. Make a name for yourself.

Being confident is what enables you to do this. If you feel less confident, identify why that is and fix it. Could it be that you don't put in enough effort? Do you show up as your full self? Are you showing up at all? Do you take appropriate risks and trust your own gut feelings? If not, when, and where did your confidence become broken? Is there more inner work to be done? Do you need a new wardrobe? Do you need to find a new hairstylist or learn to do your own hair? Sis, you might just need to put on some lip gloss. Some of these things may sound superficial, but they all matter. They all dictate how you show up and how you feel when you do. They also dictate how other people see and treat you.

You can be the most beautiful, intelligent woman in the world, but if you don't realize it and feel it for yourself, it doesn't really matter. You must know who you are and all your capabilities. First and foremost, you must know what God says about you. My Bible tells me that I am the head and not the tail, I am above and never beneath, I am the righteousness of God, He is always with me, He has plans for me, I am healed, strong, loved, forgiven and whole. You must believe that. My hope is that you come to know yourself on a deeper level and be able to see yourself how God has always seen you.

In my book, *Believe In Your Purpose: A Guide to Becoming a Successful Purpose Driven Entrepreneur,* I talk about identifying your purpose, committing to your journey, and changing your mindset. Those things are critical to your success as you navigate life, in general. It doesn't just apply to entrepreneurship. Knowing who you are and why you're here, and then committing to the process of walking that out, is the best thing that you can do for yourself. It starts with a changed mind. You will only ever do what you can first think and see with your spiritual eyes. What do you currently think and see in your future?

The steps that you take today will determine what that future looks like. If you don't like your current circumstances, you can do something about it. What you do will be based on what you would like to change. For you, that could be discovering a passion that you can get involved with, getting a certification, starting a degree program, moving to a new area or new home, applying for a new job, starting a business, writing a book, saving more than you spend, reading your Bible more, joining a church, mending a broken relationship, being more social, etc. The list can go on and on because we are all different and have different areas of need and improvement.

My area was creating a social life and being able to see beyond just being a mother. Giving my best is important and always will be. However, I had lost myself in parenting. I think most parents can relate. I rarely did anything that did not involve my children. To be honest, I was actually not upset at that. I enjoy my little ones and love being with them. I just knew that if I didn't take time to breathe and connect with myself and other people, there would be a breaking point. Regardless of how much I love them, caring for people, even your children, is still work. From every job, you need a break. I needed to go out and be social again. I needed to find ways to incorporate spending time with other adults in my life for my personal happiness.

A few months ago, I traveled to Bahamas and did not take my children. I left them in their grandmother's care and was on my merry way. I had a great time connecting with grown folks and just having fun as Shannon, not mommy. I am so looking forward to the next trip and the next and the next because there will be plenty as long as grandma agrees. I need that time to focus on just me. This is why it's important to have people who you can rely on and trust with your children. I have a very short list of these people. When I came home, both of my children were still alive and yours will be too.

I can not be the best version of myself if I don't know myself, take care of myself and honor myself. On top of that, I can only give the world what's in my capacity. My capacity is strengthened through doing these things for me. This does not apply to just me. It is also your key to life fulfillment as well. You matter, sis. I know you're used to trying to pour from an empty cup. We were taught to do that. That's not good for you! It's not even good for those who you're trying to pour into. They aren't really getting anything.

Not A Conference Call

Another thing that we were taught was to seek approval. We were obedient children for the approval of our parents. We behaved well in school and learned as best we could for our teacher's approval. When we joined a church, we behaved in a certain way for the approval of the Elders and Pastors. We cared about what everyone thought about us. There is nothing wrong with this to a degree. Overall, these actions helped us in life.

I know you're used to trying to pour from an empty cup.

However, we did them for the wrong reasons. When it gets to the point that you care more about what people think over how you feel, it is a problem. It's an even bigger problem when you care more about how you look to others than what God told you to do.

When God spoke to you, it was a one-on-one conversation. It was not a conference call with your people. So, there will be times when they don't understand your life decisions. That is ok. The only one who needs to approve is God. You move and do when He says to move and do. When I decided to take my daughter out of school to educate her at home, my mother was unsure. She ultimately supported my decision, but I could tell she wasn't on board immediately. I'm sure she was just trying to figure out how I was going to financially manage it. Afterall, I had just bought a house months before.

My mother didn't say too much, but as a mom, she wanted to know the plan. I explained it to her, and she agreed, but it was clear that she was nervous for me. She did not try to discourage me at all, but she did offer some alternatives. I understood her position as a mother, and she understood mine. In those moments, we were two mothers concerned for our children. Without hesitation, I put everything on hold and took my daughter out of school. I had already prayed about it and knew that this was best for her at the time. Things are going great. I'm even going to homeschool my other daughter once she finishes elementary school.

If I had let my mother's hesitance steer me in a different direction, I would be stressed out every day worrying about my daughter being in school with the same issues. We are at peace. Sometimes it's hard to go against what you think someone wants you to do, especially when they have a valid point, and you know that the person loves you and would only add input that they feel is in your best interest. No way would my mother try to take me out of the Will of God. No way would she try to discourage me from doing what is best for my children. I know that! Still, I had to do what I know God said and ignore her initial reaction. She is still my biggest cheerleader and support system. We talk about homeschooling challenges and wins often.

There will be times that you have to stand by yourself. There will be times when you are the only one who believes what God told you. I know I have done plenty of things that have made my mama nervous. I'm probably her favorite topic to discuss with the Lord. I know she stays on her knees in prayer having me as child. I am out there! I think real big. I do whatever I feel in the moment if I feel like God said it. I don't think about negative consequences. In my mind only positive outcomes are possible when following the leadership of the Lord. So, I just jump!

I have crazy faith! Not everyone is this way and that's ok. It doesn't mean that you have less faith than I do. It's really just having a different temperament and having a different personality type. However, I encourage you to just do something wild one time! Pray about it and take the leap! You have to get out of the box sometimes to get what you want. You were not created to be mediocre. We are called to do extraordinary things and we can. You're not basic! Stop acting like a basic chick!

I have never felt like I fit in anywhere. That is not a bad thing. It just means that I had to learn to be comfortable with myself at an early age. This does not mean that I don't feel loved or wanted. I have an amazing family and many close friends. I just always feel like I am different from everyone. Like, if everyone chooses A, I'm choosing B every single time. Being that person who is always on the outside takes confidence. Not going with the flow is not always comfortable and it will test you. I can honestly say that I always stay true to myself.

Don't try to fit where you don't need to. Stop bending and squeezing yourself into spaces that aren't for you. Create your own space. Be in your own lane. Your decisions don't require a group. There should be people who can speak into your life and get your attention. Choose those people super wisely. Make sure they hear from the Lord. When they speak, listen. While listening, also measure it against what God is saying. They should have that understanding and lead you back to God also. Anyone who tries to be the ultimate authority in your life, should probably not be speaking over your life. At the end of the day, you have to live with your choices.

Pay Attention!

We face so many distractions daily. Every time you turn around there is a new scandal playing out on social media, an unexpected event occurring in our personal lives, or someone calls us and unloads all their problems. It is not difficult to get caught up and distracted from your purpose and plans. We must make wiser decisions about how we spend our time, what we are entertained by and what we allow in. I went through a reality tv phase. I watched every reality show ever made. Never missed an episode. Then one day, I thought about how much time these shows took from me and how my energy was spent. These shows could change my mood and how I viewed the world. Please don't think that just because you are grown that you can't be influenced.

When we think about influence, we often think about young people. In reality, any of us can be influenced if we give enough attention to a thing. Watching people on social media or too much tv can have you wanting things that you didn't want before, such as new cars, bigger homes, expensive clothes etc. Then you start to be distracted by the desire for those things to the point that you start to create goals that are so far from your purpose and what you should be focusing on. These things have taken over. What happens to your original plans, the plan that God set before you? It gets put on a back burner while you chase foolishness.

Maybe that's not your issue. Maybe you let life distract you. Every little thing that happens throws you off and you feel like you have to keep starting over. You're constantly regrouping, taking a pause, or putting things on ice until you get over yet another hump. Life is always happening and the potential for life to create a distraction is always present. You need to decide how far off course you will allow these things to take you. It's natural to have to catch your breath, but that shouldn't always mean weeks of doing nothing and then starting from scratch.

Sometimes starting over is so much of a distraction that you just do something completely different. Not having completed something the first time feels like a failure and instead of facing that, you prefer to try something new. This never leads to anything other than a cycle of more of the same. Someone reading this has done this a million times. It's time to finally move forward. Some of you are in this cycle because you are afraid to fail. So, you trick yourself into never giving anything an honest try. Are you welcoming distractions, so you don't have to do anything? Only you know that answer.

Little Brown Girls

You becoming the best version of yourself is so important because little brown girls need to see that. They need to experience that. Whether you have children of your own or not, is not the point. Haven't you been motivated or influenced by a black woman other than your own mother? They will be too. What we show them is what they will be. Our children have odds stacked against them, both girls and boys, just because of the color of their skin. How they view themselves, the uniqueness of their beauty and their contribution to the world, is largely dependent on us and what we do, as I mentioned in chapter one.

We have to teach our children that regardless of how the outside world sees them and how people will try to stop their excellence from developing, that God is for them. Therefore, whatever is against them cannot prevail. We always win! The only way to make them believe that is to believe it ourselves and let our actions align with that. We must continue to break barriers and walk in our strength for these children. Whatever may be stopping you from doing that needs to be addressed so that you can be a demonstration of God's grace in your life.

This is your responsibility regardless, but especially if you are a mother. This is why I am so careful about what my children experience. I show my children that though I may be weak at times, God is strong, and

I can lean on Him and find strength. So, I am not pretending like I am never weak. I am teaching them where to take their weakness. Why? I do this because I don't want them thinking that they have to be strong all the time. I want them to be in tune with how they actually feel, not how they are told to feel. I'm not raising them with that same narrative that was put on most of us by the outside world.

I teach my children that we can have anything if we ask God for it, believe, and do what is required of us. I don't let them believe that everything will come easy or that the things that we want just fall out of the sky. I demonstrate for them how to trust and believe God for something, follow instructions, do the work and receive it. They have seen me do this many times. I had many conversations with my children about buying them a new house before it actually happened. They watched this process and were in it with me. I do that with everything.

My children know that I am in school and why. They understand the importance of education and advancement within a career. They see me doing business. They go to my website, read the information, and ask questions. When I have coaching calls with clients, I tell them what I am doing. I want them to see me managing the house, taking care of them, and working as an entrepreneur. I want them to know that they can do the same thing if they want to and yes, I also

I do this because I don't want them thinking that they have to be strong all the time.

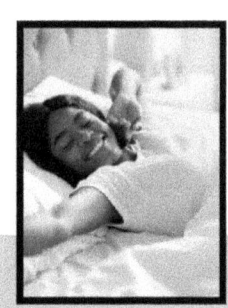

teach them the importance and value of having a life partner to do all these things with.

They understand how to save money for things that they want. They are developing a healthy relationship with money. They know when to give and are tithers. My children have so much money in their little banks because they don't spend it. They have better money habits than I do. I am so looking forward to helping them to start businesses because they have shown interest. Would that interest be there had I not included them in what I do? Probably not at this young age. They have an advantage in being my children.

Don't you want to give your children that advantage? We all know people who instead of being given an advantage, were given the short end of the stick. Some of those people have worked really hard to dig their way out of that and have made something of themselves. Others have not done quite as well. We should always want our children to do better than we did. I will never understand parents who have the means to provide, but prefer their children get it out the mud as some form of teaching life skills. It's really sickening.

Where did this concept of making children struggle to teach them come from? Who came up with this? I really struggle to understand this mentality. The only explanation that I can come up with is that the parent had a struggle life and became successful. So, they think their success is partly due to their struggle. I don't know and I really don't want to know. My main reason for wanting to be a success is so that I can provide for my children and give them a good life. Is there a reason better? Not in my book!

My children are going to have everything that I didn't have. They aren't paying for college or taking out loans. They will have cars as teenagers if they are responsible enough and ready for that. I am going to help them to purchase their homes when the time comes. They will not have a struggle life! They will know responsibility and they will know how to manage money and take care of themselves. They will be responsible adults. That doesn't have to come from struggling. Why are y'all doing that to these children?

If you have had this mentality, it's not too late to change it. Love on your babies and let them enjoy the fact that their mom is awesome and can provide for them. You also may need to get away from people with the struggle so deeply ingrained in them because they will tell you that you are spoiling your children and try to dictate what you do. Cut that off! A person who thinks like that will have you taking ten steps back in so many different areas of your life. Your goal is to set the foundation for your children's future success so that they can grow and become the future fearless face of black excellence!

The Power of Affirmations

Fear can cause us to shrink back, remain silent, hide, back down, agree when we don't mean it, stress, feel anxious, and experience an array of negative emotions and feelings. Ask me how I know. It all really starts with how you feel about yourself. I have been able to overcome all of this and to be the fearless person that I am today, who does not care about opinions, naysayers, or haters, through positive affirmations and prayer. I am going to share with you twenty-five affirmations that I tell myself on a regular basis.

Sit with these affirmations for a while. Think about how they make you feel. Add some of your own that mean something to you. Let them sink in. Believe them! Use them in battle along with your other tools. This simple action step will make a huge difference and have a major impact on your life. It will change how you see yourself, how you talk to yourself and what you believe you can do and have. It will cause you to attract to yourself whatever you want for your life. I can't wait to hear your testimonies. Please share them with me by email.

Daily Affirmations

1. I am worthy

2. I am healed

3. I am beautiful

4. I am confident

5. I am strong

6. I am more than a conqueror

7. I am smart

8. I am capable

9. I am a good mother

10. I am loved

11. I am special

12. I am powerful

13. I communicate well

14. I can do all things through Christ

15. I am a good person

16. I can accept a compliment

17. I am bold

18. I do my own thing

19. I make good decisions

20. I am a friend of God

21. I have accomplished a lot

22. My potential is endless

23. I can't be stopped

24. I am more than good enough

25. I am fearless

About The Author

Shannon Wilkerson, a former educator, has been a cheerleader and coach for women for over fifteen years. She is certified in life coaching as well as leadership and business. She has helped countless clients to grow in the areas of personal and professional development and to write best-selling books. She is a motivational speaker and an accomplished author. Her book titles include *"Believe In Your Purpose: A Guide to Becoming A Successful Purpose Driven Entrepreneur"* and *"To My Girls: A Look At Friendship From The Perspective of Eight Women"*. She has also been a ghostwriter for many projects that you may be familiar with.

After a long career supporting women with their personal and professional goals and meeting many brilliant women along the way, Shannon is looking forward to one day hosting a major conference and retreat to bring these powerhouse women together. Another goal close to her heart is creating a series of anthologies including stories of triumph that can encourage and uplift women around the globe. So, stay tuned for what is to come. It's going to be amazing!

Shannon loves to hear feedback from those who enjoy her work and people who would like to connect further. She can be contacted through most social media platforms under her own name and through her website at shanniwilke.com.

www.ingramcontent.com/pod-product-compliance
Lightning Source LLC
Chambersburg PA
CBHW051222120626
46547CB00013B/1468